GRANDMA JULIA

by

Ann Y. Tyler

This book is based on the writings of Julia May Jones Eastman. Some minor editing has occurred for improved clarity. Much of the original dialect and spelling (or misspelling) has remained unchanged.

GRANDMA JULIA
Copyright © 2013 by Ann Y. Tyler. All rights reserved, including the right to reproduce this book, or portions thereof, in any form. No part of this text may be reproduced, transmitted, downloaded, decompiled, reverse engineered, or stored in or introduced into any information storage and retrieval system, in any form or by any means, whether electronic or mechanical without the express written permission of the author. The scanning, uploading, and distribution of this book via the Internet or via any other means without the permission of the publisher is illegal and punishable by law. Please purchase only authorized electronic editions and do not participate in or encourage electronic piracy of copyrighted materials.

The publisher does not have any control over and does not assume any responsibility for author or third-party websites or their content.

Cover designed by Telemachus Press, LLC

Cover photo is author Ann Tyler as a baby with Grandma Julia May Jones Eastman

Cover art:
Copyright © iStockphoto/5137561/Old-Book/Ivan Bajic
Copyright © iStockphoto/18259969/bananahuman

Cover and Interior photographs are from family collections and are reprinted with permission.

Published by Telemachus Press, LLC
http://www.telemachuspress.com

Mail Author at:
Ann Y. Tyler
P. O. Box 420668
Kissimmee, FL 34742-0668

ISBN: 978-1-942899-37-2 (eBook)
ISBN: 978-1-942899-38-9 (Paperback)

Version 2018.11.06

10 9 8 7 6 5 4 3 2

A poignant reminder of our route from the time our ancestors stepped off slave ships onto American soil; without benefit of reading or writing a language new to them, but creating an extensive oral history through to the mid-Twentieth Century; passed on courtesy of the determined woman who set pen to paper during the 1950s, and her granddaughter, Dr. Ann Tyler, who has collected Grandma Julia's journals, edited them, and let them live again. Brava, Dr. T!
~Chassie West, Author of *The Leigh Ann Warren Mysteries*

Grandma Julia is a masterful work of literary art—a perceptive and piquant telling of American history insightfully captured in the written prose of Julia May Jones Eastman. Her granddaughter, Dr. Ann Y. Tyler, has carefully conveyed the sagacity, soul, strength, struggle, and sacrifice of this family through which we learn a bit more of our history…the black, the white, and the red…the truth.
~Rev. Dr. Cynthia Hinson Graham, Author of *Help! It Still Hurts*

Table of Contents

Foreword i
Acknowledgments v

Chapter 1 Of the Lineage of Julia Jones Eastman 1
Chapter 2 Of Great Grandma Winna 4
Chapter 3 G. Grand Uncle's Friendship 15
Chapter 4 Kheenee Sioux Comes to Ask for Winna 24
Chapter 5 The Mistress Has a Talk with Winna 27
Chapter 6 Back to Kheenee Sioux 31
Chapter 7 Listening into Pandora's Box 42
Chapter 8 In Diversion & The Huntsmen 46
Chapter 9 The Grapevine Telegraph 49
Chapter 10 A Discovery 51
Chapter 11 Winna's Trial and Punishment 54
Chapter 12 Grandfather—"Big Ellec"—Alexander Sioux
   Robinson 60
Chapter 13 1833 A. D.—Courtship and Marriage 66
Chapter 14 Ann's Afterthoughts 73

Family Photos 77
Appendix A Aunt Candace's Poem 93
Glossary for This Edition's Slave Dialect 95
Index 103

Grandma Julia

FOREWORD

"Meda, meda, bentay!" She called us from the street to get us ready for our parents to pick us up from work. Getting ready meant from Monday through Friday we ate fresh-baked peanut butter cookies and daily drank a different flavor of Kool-Aid in 6 oz. Dixie paper cups. This dark-chocolate-ample-hipped-warm-full-bosomed woman took care of us, me and my cousins and a couple of our Puerto Rican school friends who lived in the block, every afternoon after a glorious day at our neighborhood elementary school. I did not find out 'til years later when my daughter was taking high school Spanish that my Grandma Julia was saying, "¡Mira, mira, vente," which meant, "Look, look, come," or colloquially speaking, "Looka heah [here], now, come on in the house!" We just knew that it was time to come in the house, pronto!

When her son, my uncle, Julius Dunbar Eastman, decided in 1971 to take on a writing project involving Grandma's writings, he said to me, "Alright Junie, this project will be continued by you and David," who was my first cousin and son of Esther who was Grandma Julia's daughter and Uncle Julius' sister. I answered, hesitantly, not wanting to hurt his feelings, "Well, OK, Uncle Julius." He went on to Glory in October, 2010. Now here I am at age 75, a big procrastinator, continuing Edyth's Lineage with an experience-filled book of Grandma Julia's writings, transcribed from the bound pages in her own handwriting from her b/w Sterling NOTE BOOK. The front cover has printed on it, "Property of 'No 1 A'", and on the second line it says, "School_____".

All this time I assumed that only Grandma Julia's writings were inside the Notebook. Today, Sunday, September 15, 2013, I found the writings of my Aunt Candace Yvette Eastman, Grandma Julia's youngest daughter, after whom I am named. Her poetry was written when she was in the seventh and eighth grades in the Bronx. I knew she had written poetry when she was an adult, but not when she was in junior high school. I am afraid to turn the pages, too fast. They are slightly yellowed and Grandma had inscribed in her beautiful, flowing, cursive handwriting on the inside cover, "Mrs. P. W. Eastman, Sr. A. D. 1952–3–4." Well, Grandma was writing while I was beginning my sojourn at the High School of Music & Art in Manhattan, located at that time on "THE HILL"; 102 steps leading up to Convent Avenue and 135th Street. The Bagel Man sold delicious product at the bottom of the steps, daily until way after I graduated in June, 1955.

Aunt Candace's poetry pages were held together with a large, triangular paper clip, which I have since replaced with a smaller, newer paper clip. One of her poems is in Appendix A. Aunt Candace was in 7B[1] in the '30s. Amazingly to me I landed in 7SP1 at Herman Ridder Junior High School in the '50s. I have kept these writings inside the Grandma's Notebook, placed inside a large quart sized Ziploc plastic bag. I am going to seek advice about preservation methods and carefully Xerox the old pages.

At the top of each and every notebook page of the stories, on the left side of the thin red margin line, Grandma Julia had written *"continued from p"*. That phrase will not be shown in the manuscript after *p. a3*. The numbers were circled from a circle 1, until she switched to using parentheses at "a(7)". On the top right corner, Uncle Julius had written, in his plain engineering style, a plain, precise 2, as well on the subsequent pages of his mother's Sterling Note Books. He stopped at 95 in Book No 1 A which was the beginning of one of Grandma Julia's anecdotal stories, Kheenee Sioux and Winna, Julia's Great-Grandma. The majority of Grandma Julia's words, varied spellings, grammatical syntax, punctuation and spelling, especially of all the nicknames, are transcribed as is, unabridged, typed directly from her lovely, flowing handwriting on the pages.

For clarity there will be corrections for a few phrases noted in brackets [ ]: spelling, punctuation, capitalization, dialect, creating chapter titles in addition to Julia's, and inserted paragraph indents. There are few changes regarding her grammatical style in order to keep the flow of her written thoughts.

ACKNOWLEDGMENTS

MY FIRST NETWORK included my late parents, Philip Walter Eastman, Jr. and Dr. Anna Byrd Eastman Wheaton. Since age 14 I heard my Dad and the late Carl Diton, my piano teacher refer to me almost every week, "Dr. Eastman …" this, and "Dr. Eastman …" that. I hope they were both looking on in May of 2002 when I received the Doctorate of Curriculum & Instruction at the University of Central Florida. My Mom, at age 91, daughter and friends were there rejoicing for me. She gave me my first piano lessons sitting by her side on our piano bench when I was four years old. As I approached my senior year at Manhattan's High School of Music & Art, I heard my Mom put her foot down with Dad about me going south to college to "get some quality education and Negro Culture." Dad expressed his concern for finding the money and, that the NY schools were cheaper. Being accepted at Oberlin in Ohio and Hunter College in NY, as well as Howard University in Washington, D. C., had me looking forward to getting away from home.

Amazingly, several years after Howard's Commencement I learned that Mom had practically depleted her Retirement Fund to send me to Howard thereby supplementing my tuition scholarship and Dad's loans from the "loan sharks". Who knew that my determined decision to switch from Music Education to Drama would be subtly and completely thwarted by my English Professor, Dr. Bracey. When I confided in her, she listened, smiled and said, "Ann, I have enjoyed your performances with the Howard Players. I hope that you would share your other excellent gift of teaching. The children need teachers like you." Thank you, Dr. Bracey.

This final challenge came from my late Uncle Julius Dunbar Eastman, Sr. He threw down the gauntlet to me, his son and his nephew, my first cousins, after he meticulously compiled, edited his mother's ancestral writings, created charts, arranged family photos and published *The Lineage of EDYTH* in 1971. I felt honored that he would assign this task to me as if I were one of his math or engineering students. He was an example to me as I watched him study for ten years, one course at a time while working full time to become a Professional Civil Engineer in New York, mainly on Long Island. As the oldest of the three first cousins, I must still thank you, Gerry Eastman and David Lisbon for your "brotherly" encouragement and memory sharing.

I have dearly appreciated other words of advice and blessings which have come from my children, William P. Ellison-"Billy", Annette F. Ellison-"Netti", and Robert W. Tyler-"Bebop"; my precious authors and treasured friends-Chassie West, Rev. Dr. Cynthia Hinson Graham, Dr. Denise Mose, Scot

Walker, Jane Bateman, Ernestine V. Brooks and Yvonne Holmes Riggs. Kudos and gratitude go to Steven Himes with the Telemachus Press Staff, MaryAnn, Terri and Johnny.

Finally, thank you, my cherished cousin, who has always been a Big Sister for me. We grew up, Junie & Bonnie, visiting back and forth between my Bronx and her Buffalo, Dr. Ann Y. Tyler and Dr. Yvonne Scruggs-Leftwich. Throughout this project I have often asked God for help. Then I would thank Him heartily for removing the clouds of procrastination that overshadowed me many a day.

Grandma Julia

Grandma Julia with Author Ann Tyler "as a baby"

Chapter 1
Of the Lineage of Julia Jones Eastman
by Julia Jones Eastman

AGAIN AND AGAIN I have mused to myself, if there ever was a little girl who loved to listen to ancient and seemingly fictitious, yet true stories, as much as I did. From the time that I could first remember, (which by evidence, was between the third and fourth years of my life) I was always the first of the children to get my little wooden block or stool and sit very close to my mother or father which ever of them told the story, and listen with the keenest interest possible, to every least detail of it.

Now it is quite apparent that a girl who was born to parents just 18 years after their Emancipation, could only have such tales told to her as pertained to the narrow, (or yet in a way, wide,) environment of a slave's existence.

Of all the stories told to me, which were many and varied in topics, I took special interest in the tales of our personal family concern. And since there was no history about the personal accomplishment or achievement of the black race of America, a descendant could only learn their lineage or ancestors through an oral or spoken narrative of events.

The first character of one of the stories of which I will give an account is my Great-Great-Grandma of the lineage of my mother. As I have mentioned above, these stories were told to us by our parents, most generally by our mother, Ciney, about our G. G. Grandmother whose name was Edith, (Eady for short), it was very little to tell. Ma said that all she knew about G. G. Grandmother was what she heard her Grandma tell after the day's work was finished and the family (which consisted of 1st, G. G. Ma Winna, I learned that Winna stood for "Rowina" or "Wenna", G. G. uncle Willa, brother to Winna, G. Ma Easter, G. Dad Ellic Sioux and the three children, Ellec Sioux, Jr.; Henderson and Chenne, Ciney for short), would be comfortably seated around the fire side of one of the log cabins on the plantation. G. G. Grandma Winna was not very old, so goes the legend, when she died, and the most that G. Gra. Ma Winna could remember about her was that she longed for the time when she might go back to the homeland of pappy. She knew very little of her Mammy Edyth whom she use to say was taken away from pappy by some big pale faced men and they never saw her anymore. She lived in the hope that someday she would go back to the wonderful homeland of her mammy & pappy. On her wrists and ankles were hard ringlike scars which was the result of the chains which were used when she was forced with other Africans to leave the homeland, to chain them hands and feet in the rafts until they got them a far distance out in the big water and then they were herded, like animals in a big ship bound for lands which were both unknown and unheard of by them.

The Savages who stole them did have enough human thought for them, to separate males from females. It was in this way that she lost forever her homeland-mate or husband. On her right shoulder was three stripes or molds which marked each year she had been the wife of her mate, whether the raft that brought him to the big ship was destroyed or sent to another ship besides the one to which she was taken she never knew. One great consolation was she was allowed to have strapped to her, her two babes, a boy and a girl. The boy named Willa was branded with 3 dots or spots which marked the years, and the girl named Winna had not yet been branded. So from this time on their ages were reckoned by their owners in the U. S. A. in the State of Virginia. G. Grandma Winna says G. G. Grandma Edith's work was looking after the eggs and young hatchlings in the chicken yards. Little besides this is not known of G. G. Grandma Edith. She was buried in the Slave Cemetery somewhere in the state of Virginia in the County of Brunswick on the plantations of Robinson & Smith, combined through the alliance of marriage.

~ // ~

Chapter 2
Of Great Grandma Winna

THE STORY IS somewhat longer and in a fuller detail of memory! As she, (before she was too old to lose interest) use to talk of her life often and fluently. And, added to her lineal history was quite a lot told by my grandfather, I can remember my G. father. Great G. Ma's story began at the time when she first could remember was that she and her little brother used to live in a little log cabin, on the Robinson-Smith plantation, with their Mammy, who called her by the name of Winna, and called her brother by the name of Willa, and of course, as was the fad of most of the Va. slaves they adopted the names of their owner, therefore G. G. Grandma's family used the name of Robinson.

Having been taken or stolen from everything, but her two babes, that was near and dear to her, I can imagine that my poor G. G. Grandma was strongly endeared to Willa and Winna. Lucky for her and the babes, that she was assigned to a duty which kept her always situated so that she could have them near her.

Sometime during the Years
After G. G. Grandma's death, G. Grandma Winna was taken into the kitchen as an apprentice for the art of cooking, and G. Granduncle Willa was assigned to keeping the supply of wood for the different chambers of the great house and for the kitchen. Which was lucky for them again since their duties placed them where they could daily come in contact with one another. Now, owing to the fact that these babes were her only source of endearment and love, G. G. Grandma kept them so bound to her for love & comfort that it somewhat held them away from the free association with other children. And for this reason, Great Grand Ma, except for her brother and one or two girlfriends, did not get out with the plantation girls much. By the way G. Grandma, after G. G. Grandma's death was placed in the cabin with an old woman who was exempted from duty but just the picking of seed from cotton lint when she felt like it. And her brother still lived in their mother's cabin.

I have so many many times wished that I had the pictures of all my ancestors that I have heard "tell" about. If I live long enough I Shall try to draw a mind picture from imagination, the pictures of my ancestors as they were described to me. My G. G. Grandma was not pictured, but my G. Grandma was described as having an oval sloped face, not too thick lips, with a mouth not negroidly wide. Very thick head of hair and not grey Even at a very ripe old age. not too slim yet not a fat person. about 5 feet 10 at the age of 20 which she use to say she was that size at 16.

She was chosen as cook number one in the kitchen of the great house when she was twenty one, and also the confidant of the household. So far as the cookery was concerned, having the privileged duty to issue out and order in all, foods for selected menues. Under her were two other girls as apprentice cooks—she did all cooking on Saturday for Sunday. The slaves were not to do any work on Sunday, not unless an immergency about the farm products arose like saving fodder out of the rain or setting plants just after a good rain. Under those circumstances all field hands were set to work even on Sundays. So G. Grandma with her two kitchen mates and G. Grand uncle Willa use to go fishing for their own pleasure; Since they did not care for church and I guess I knew less, poor dears. Well God protects the ignorant. After quite a length of time, G. Grandma Wina had under her supervision about four or five helpers in the kitchen: So much so that she could leave them the duty of preparing the meals quite often while she took some free time off.

In the Month of May, one day, after putting everything in order and giving the needed instructions to her aids, She scampered off through the shady woods down to one of their brooks or big branches, to sit in the shade and do some knitting on a pair of socks which she had started for one of the young masters. While busily counting, and knitting three, and purling three, she noticed a rippling in the water as it flowed by. She, thinking it to be a fish or frog in the water, kept on knitting, purling three, and knitting three. By the by, she lay down her knitting and sat, watching the water flow. In the stillness of the stream she saw, as looking in a mirror, the reflection of the trees, from the opposite side of the stream, in the water. And to her amazing fright in the top of the tree was the appearance of a man having broad shoulders and a full cape of straight hair which reached far below his shoulders. Frightened more than if she had seen a rattlesnake without remembering her knitting or anything else, she made a deer bound for the great house. When she came up to the cabins her brother was there with some more of the house servants. And seeing a strange look on her face, quickly came up to her and asked anxiously "What fo you been skert?" She was still too tired and shocked to explain so she only said, "Nuffin." But the experience of this event never left Wina's mind and the feature of the tree man was forever stamped upon her memory. However she kept it a secret to herself since it seemed to awaken something within her that she had not quite experienced before. Those eyes so deep and meaningful and full of questions and to her so strange yet strikingly appealing.

For the next two or three weeks Winna went about her work, living over and over, each day, the shocking, but pleasant experience down by the Big Branch or Creek. At last one Sunday She, her brother, and a couple of other girls went down to the *Big Branch's Valley to spend the day at fishing. *Note here that G. G. Dad Ken [Kheenee Sioux] told G. G. Ma Wina that he had been down to that branch every day since he first saw her hoping each time to see her again. As every one reached the banks of the stream they chose their fishing seat some distance apart so that they would not talk and frighten the fish away. Winna as was her wont, went up stream about a stones throw away from the rest of the group, fixed a nice seat with a pile of brush and sticks and sat down to fish. After about a quarter hour she noticed that her fish line moved a bit but thinking it to have been caused by a rippling in the water She did not pay much attention to it. A few more moments, and to her utter astonishment and surprise, there was stretched out on a large limb, which reach almost across the stream, the same being who had so thoroughly frightened her before. A quiet impulse to whistle for the rest of her group came over her, and then, in the flash of seconds, she thought to do other: steadily gazing at her object of astonishment she began contemplating what to say or do. Then all at once his face was moved as the rolling back of a stage curtain, and a big broad, open mouthed smile broke forth which lightened up his countenance, and a perfect set of strong white teeth were displayed. At this gesture of friendly introduction, Winna, before she could conceal or control here state of happiness, ventured to smile back; and at the same time she made a move to get up from her seat to join the rest of her group. but in getting up she stepped on a piece of stick which gave a roll and down in the stream she tumbled. At this dreadful happening she was too frightened to refuse the help, which when she did not realize it, she had been thrown face downward straight up and down the back of a strong armed red man who was wading downstream to where her friends were seated.

Holding her two hands under his chin, with one hand, while with the other hand he paddled himself downstream with her head resting on his mop of wet hair just between his shoulder and side of his face. As he pulled up on the bank of the stream her brother Willa grabbed both him and her and excitingly exclaiming, 'What yo done? What yo done to Winna!?' The Indian, (It was an indian who had rescued her) said nothing. He flung Winna on the ground and going over to where a tree had fallen he cleared away the brush, came over to where her limp form lay and, taking hold of her shoulders he motioned to her brother Willa to take her feet, which he did without asking any questions. Quickly they laid her across the trunk of the tree, face downward, and the Indian, pressing gently and firm on her back in some way caused Winna to get her breath again. She groaned; "Pull em down" said the Indian, motioning to Willa to take her off the tree trunk and lay her flat on the ground. He then suggested that the girls who were with her to take off Winna's wet clothes, and divide some of their dry clothes with her until hers could dry.

While the girls were taking care of Winna, He had Willa to go upstream with him that he may show him where and how Winna met with her accident.

It has never been told what else the Indian and Willa talked about, but from that day on they became fast simpathetic friends. When they came back to where the girls were, they had divided their dry clothes with Winna and she was lying resting peacefully upon a bed of leaves which the girls had raked together and covered with one of their aprons. Her wet clothing were hung on some shrubbery by the stream.

The girls, I must note, had also become better acquainted with Winna's affairs of the accident, which caused a very interesting air of seek and find out among the whole group.

Well it was about lunch time and as the main attendent was indisposed, the other two girls busied themselves getting out the lunch, while Willa went down to the Spring, in the stream, to fetch a pail of water.

Getting Acquainted—It was during this space of time that the Indian, who was ever looking her way, quietly went over to where Winna lay and kneeling down he made another one of those broad smiles, only this time it matured into a big grin. At which Winna turned her face away to hide, from him, the pleasure that she was quite sure was being registered on her face. The Indian reached over and drew her face directly facing his gaze. This time the grin was gone and his face wore an eager, stern expression which made Winna wince. She even felt a little uneasy. For about 10 seconds he just looked at her as if to try to read her mind through her face. Then, without anything more said or implied, he asked her, "Who be you?" This came so quick and sudden that Winna had not time to think before she quickly answered, "Winna." At this he reached into his coat of bearskin and gave her a little sack with something inside, and walked around to the other side of the bed, took from his pocket a pair of snips came close to the bed and quicker that one could close and open the eye he had snipped of a small braid of her hair and put it in the same pocket from which he had taken the pouch he gave her, and displaying that broad grin again he turned went over to the banks of the big stream and dove in and out of sight. Winna screamed! This brought the girls with Willa over to her pallet.

"What fo you squeling Winna?" asked Willa.

"Didn't yo see redman jump in de watah?" moaned Winna.

"Wal what is dat to call out de blood hounds wit?" asked Willa. "De man is gone home."

"Wal," said Winna, "Ah didn't tell him ah was glad he pulled me out de watah."

"Dats nuffin," said Willa, "yo is got plenty nuf time ef yo sees im agin." But Winna was not so sure that she would ever see Redman again. She reached under her pillow of leaves and gently fumbled with the little deerskin pouch he had given her, and wondered to herself, what fo he gave it her and what could be inside of it.

As the rest of the group sat down on the leaves and grass to eat, they called to her to come over and join them. This she refused with the excuse that she had rather rest until time to start back home. While they ate she turned her back to them and inspected the pouch from the outside but decided to not open it until she got back to the great house and hide herself in her own little cabin room where no one could disturb her. She got up from the pallet, and went over to the shrubbery and got her clothes, which was dry by this time, and redressed, returning her friends back their clothes.

When they got back to the great house they did their different chores, then went to the cabin for the night. Granny Lena, as they used to call the old lady with whom Winna lived, sleeping inside the cabin; so to keep from disturbing her they sat outside in the yard, until bed time, and talked of the events of the day. Winna did not do much talking with them, as her thoughts were fully taken up with new happenings in her life. Willa, knowing that he must be up bright and early to start the fire in the kitchen, went early to bed. And so did the other two girls. With her big eyes wide, and hands a little shakey, Winna when she realized she was alone, did not awaken Grany Lena, She went softly to her room and pulled the pretty homespun drape, which had been spun and dyed by her own Mommy Edith, across the door, and lit her tallow candle and sat down in the middle of the floor with the first real Santa Claus She had had since Mommy Edith died. With shaking hands and pounding heart She drew the pouch down from her bosom and cautiously untied the string, which was also made from some of the same skin as the pouch was and dumped the contents of the pouch into her lap. The first thing which attracted her attention was her knitting, which she had taken with her to the stream nearly a month before. "Oh," gasped Winna softly, "he is de tree man dat I saw befo! Cause dis is my marsa's socks dat I woz knitting."

The next thing which took hold of her elated attention was a minature heart shaped, open face frame, woven from some of the wool with which she was knitting her masters sock, and interwoven within the frame was a wisp of coarse straight black hair. And in the center of the heart shaped frame of hair were two words scrawled. She could not read poor thing. So it was quite sometime before Wina learned what those two words were. Their identification which we will speak of in a later Chapter.

[Ed. This Description is from Grandma Julia's Book #a1, page 93.]

Now concerning the locket spoken of, Kheenee Sioux had gone back, after he had rescued Winna from drowning, to the spot where she fell in the stream and picked up the socks which Winna was knitting and carried them to his Wigwam and used some of the thread, with which she was knitting and intertwined it with a thread like wisp of his hair and had fastened it, in a heart-shaped figure, to a 4 inch square piece of chamois skin, and in the center of the heart was engraved the two words—Kheenee Sioux.—Which when he had asked Winna her name, and had obtained a wisp of her hair, he went to his Wig. and made another locket in the same shape and size as the one he had given Winna, and in the center was the word—Winna—. The next time he saw Winna he asked her to let him have the ensign he had given her so that he could weave the two together. She had him unfasten it at the back and slip it from her bosom over which she wore it continually.

He took them home and wove them together and brought them back and gave them to her. Winna asked him why he had made this beautiful thing and given it to her. To which he answered, as he drew Winna close to him, "It mean that in our hearts our love for you and me everlasting and sure, growing intertwined, and never ending so long as you and I shall live."

Then with a lover's embrace that only an American Indian can give, he placed it over Winna's breast and fastened it at the back, and requested her to keep it always in memory of their love. To which Great Grandma Winna, so the legend goes, promised to do, and reaching up, encircled his shoulders with her arms, and for the first time in her life, really hugged and kissed a man without being persuaded to do so. Please let it be understood that Winna had asked Ken what the two words were which was engraved on the square in the center of the heart, and he had taken it and told her that on her side of the ensign the two words were <u>Kheenee Sioux</u> which represented his name and tribe; and on the opposite side the one word was her name—<u>Winna</u>—. This locket was placed on G. Grandma's breast when she died.

Winna had never been so happy, as she could remember, since her Mammy died. She gathered all the things together and put them in the porch and hid the pouch under her wheat straw mattress. She went to bed, but, to save her, she could not and did not sleep until the first hours of day dawn. When it was light enough for the rooster to come out of the roost into the yard, Winna was up and dressed, and washed her face and combed her hair, and scanned with delightful pride, the place from which the tree man had clipped the braid of hair.

Lena and Jane, two of the assistant cooks, came to the kitchen a short time after Winna, and with a jolly greeting, began teasing her about falling in the big creek and came near drowning. Winna, who never talked too much, only grinned and said back, joking,

"Wal fishermon ketch no fish if dere wone no baits in de watah."

Chapter 3
G. Grand Uncle's Friendship

DURING THIS NARRATION, when speaking of G. Granduncle Willa, we will say Willa for Short.

After Willa filled the wood grate in the kitchen with wood, he had little else to do. So he busied himself with cleaning up and placing the implements of the woodpile. and cleaning the menfolks boots and shoes. He, with a group of boys of the plantation, also used to go down in the lowgrounds and pull weeds of various kinds to put in the pens and stys for the calves and hogs. So when he was absent as much as one or two hours at the time from the great house, no one ever worried or suspected anything but that he was down in the lowgrounds. But not all the time was Willa spending time delving in hog and calf weeds.

One morning, long before time for him to be up and at the great house, Willa took his old hickory stick, which he use to carry about the plantation when he use to go roaming, and down through the lowgrounds and to the big branch he went. The last time he was there, the Indian gave him a whistle which he had, and instructed him that if or when he came down to the stream and did not see him he was to blow this whistle once if everything was all right and three times if trouble was with him. The Indian said he would answer with the same call that was received. If trouble, he would answer but not come, if all right, he would both answer and come. So this is how Willa and the Indian met together several times. and quite a few times Winna was with her brother.

Early May during one of the holidays, Willa and Winna ventured across the stream to the Indian's Wigwam or home. This, I am told, was really the most frightening and indeed the most thrilling days of G. Grandma Winna's life. The day was hot and sunny yet the air stirred gently, and Winna, her brother, and the Indian went, not out of the Valley, only just to the Wigwam and they wandered up and about the banks of the stream, the Indian explaining to them every herb and berry along the coast. Winna was so happy that she forgot to be shy anymore. There seemed to be a nearness of feeling that made her feel secure, even with the Indian. She even forgot that she was a slave. Now, as the noon of day approached, Willa began to think of lunch. Of course Winna was so taken up with the day that she thought nothing of her eats But, when Willa thought of it, he had left the lunch on the other side of the stream.

"Wal," said Willa, "Ah take de skif so to git de feeds."

"Yah," said the Indian, "skip."

"Willa," called out Winna, "take me wif yo."

"No no Sis, Ah be back mity soon."

"No no I go too, caus I is skert," says Winna.

"Yah you stay, Khee-nee Sioux no hurt you," said the Indian, as he came near to Winna and, at the same time, took hold of her hand. Winna stared at him wide-eyed and asked—

"Who be Khee-nee Sioux?"(This was the first time she had heard his name.)

"I be Khee-nee Sioux ..." said the Indian with an assuring grin.

At this time Willa said, "Yes Sis, poh thing, yo is safe wid Ken, he is a frin."

"Wal," said Winna, "ah stay."

At this conclusion Kheenee Sioux patted her head and hurried down to the stream to help Willa off to go across. When Willa was safe in the skiff and started to leave he looked up at the skies and exclaimed, "Uh it look mity stormy up dere. Sposen it storms and ah cant git back soon, what mought ah do!"

"Uh huh" says Ken, "take um whistle and tell me if you can if you can't, and when you will."

It must be understood that, during their short acquaintance, the Indian had taught Willa many words of language by a whistle's signature. And Willa having that keen African instinct of sign language, and also being quite eager to learn, had accomplished almost an education of signs, and herb wonders, and boat building, and bow and arrow shooting from the Indian. So he pushed off towards the other side of the stream.

Khee-nee Sioux hastened back to the wigwam and found Winna looking at the many different fur rugs which he had hung along the walls.

"Do you like um Winna?" he asked as he came close to her.

"Yah, de is mity purty and nice. Whar yo git em?"

"Fum em fox, em deer, em coons, and him," he said pointing to a real bear skin, which caused him to come close enough to her that she seemed to hear his heartbeat.

"If I didn't get him he get me. So I got him too. You want him, Winna?" he asked, placing his hand over her shoulder. Winna winced a little, then thought to herself, "He is good Red Man he wont hurt Willa's sister."

"Wal" said Winna, "Ah don want take yer purty thang fum you, whar yo Mamy?"

"Mammy gone um happy hunting ground"

"Yaa?" said Winna, "den whar yo pappy?"

"Um white man kill um."

"Wal who is yo got?" asked Winna,

"Kheenee Sioux got em bow and arrow, em skif, got em Wigwam" At this point his hand that was on Winna's shoulder slid down and facing her he drew her to him (proposal of first generations) with his usual broad grin and then said with a quick steady voice, "and now I got Winna".

"No No" said Winna "masa will Kill Winna ef he know I be wid Red man."

"Winna, Kheenee Sioux want you, Kheenee Sioux got no woman; do you want um Kheenee Sioux?"

Winna said nothing, she just stood there looking into nothingness.

Kheenee Sioux dropped down on another rug which lay on the floor, and gently but firmly pulled Winna down beside him.

"Talk to Kheenee Sioux Winna, him no hurt you." Winna still said nothing. The Indian got up, went to an old chest and opened it. It was made from rough oak boards and lined with the skin of some kind of animal. he drew from it a string of beads of many colors and holding them up he did a dance that Winna had not seen done before. (first Generation of Indian and African Way of taking a Mate.) He put the beads over his head and on his neck and danced about the wigwam then came over to Winna, took the beads from his neck and placed them on Winna's, took her by the hands lifted her from the rug and kissing both cheeks he danced around and around. All this time Winna said nothing. She was like someone paralized or stunned.

Then all of a sudden the wigwam lighted up and a sharp violent peal of thunder broke forth to such an extent that Winna lost controll of her strength and fell limp in Kheenee Sioux arms. Ken, who had many times had the experience of such electric storms, lifted Wina to his home-made lounge and laid her down gently and covered her with the bear skin rug which she had so admiringly gazed at a short time before. It turned out to be an awful terrific electric storm. When the flash of lightning and roaring of thunder, and the downpour of rain ceased, it was near to the end of the afternoon, and evening was fast approaching. The Stream had begun to swell and it rose to the overflow of its banks.

By this time Winna had become more composed, and was walking up and down in the Wigwam wondering; what has become of Willa. Ken said nothing for a while then he took some sticks of charcoal built a small fire and hung over it a squirrel which he had dried and smoked. The which was broiled done and brown by time the clouds broke and night fall put in. He roasted some corn and nuts which he took from a box and with some hot tea he made from herbs he had procured, and some Indian meal cakes. He spread out a large cloth of deer skin in front of the fire and called Winna over to eat something, as she had eaten nothing since in the early part of morning. But Winna was so worried about Willa, She had no desire for eats although she was tired and hungry however she did finally sit down on the rug and start to eat. And to her surprise she never tasted better food. And the tea had a most delightful flavor. After supper Ken persuaded her to take a small cup of Valley rum to settle her nerves. He then took down his bow and arrow and started to the door. Winna took hold of his coat tail and said,

"Don't leave Willa's sister alone. I skert in dis cabin. What fo yo take de shooting bow?"

"Me go now to call to Willa."

"Oh! I is glad!" said Winna, as her face lighted up with a glow of joy. Ken grabbed her to him and said, "My Winna she like um Sun. She good, she lovely woman."

"Let me go wid yo please Suh," coaxed Winna.

"All right, come," said Ken, and taking a whistle from his pocket he blew out one long slow peal; then, as if it had been expected, came back an answer, ditto.

"Willa is down by the bank and all right," he told Winna. He then made another complicated set of whistles, and the answer from the other side of the stream came back, ditto.

"He can't cross stream until water go down," Ken told Winna.

"What kin Winna do?" asked Winna, with wide-eyed fear, "effen Willa don come back Massa will kill Winna."

"Massa no kill Winna," sneered Ken, "Me kill um Massa."

"Oh please Suh git me back fo sunset; caus I is head Kitchen woman."

"Winna go back when water go down," said Kheenee Sioux. "Me now talk to Winna."

He made three long whistles and two short ones, and back came the answer Pu-Pu-Pu-ditto.

"Him be here when water go down. Him gone to look see at um big Wigwam."

"Thank ee Keenee Sioux," said Winna somewhat nervous but with a confidential gesture. They then went back to the wigwam and after learning more about each other, he coaxed her to lay down on his bunk and get some much needed rest. He with his bow and arrows sat on a stool outside of the door to the wigwam to listen for a call from Willa. About 10 o'clock P. M. the water began to fall and Kheenee Sioux knew from experience that it would be between four and five hours before the waters were low enough for Willa to come over, he stopped his watching and slipped inside the wigwam for a few winks of sleep too. He tipped over to the cot and saw that Winna was sleeping soundly. Kheenee Sioux fastened the skins of the door to the wigwam securely then dropped down on a rug which was on the floor in front of the lounge and was soon fast asleep. He did not calculate the length of time he slept, he realized he had been sleeping very soundly when he was awakened by a light tap-tap on the side of the wigwam. Reaching for his bow and arrows, he peered over at the couch to see if his charge was still asleep, he went stealthily to the door and peeping out through a secret peephole, he saw Willa standing in the yard by a big oak tree. He opened the door quickly and was at Willa's side asking all questions and not hardily waiting for an answer before asking again. Willa made out to stop him long enough to ask him how Winna fared: To which he beckoned to him to follow him, which Willa did and Ken lifted the curtain by the door and bid Willa look see. He grinned satisfaction at seeing her peacefully sleeping.

"Wal," says Willa, "Ah is got to waken her. It mought be anudder storm by monin."

"Can't um stay wid Kheenee Sioux Willa?" asked Ken pleadingly.

"Naw! Naw!" quothed Willa excitedly, "us massa will kill my sissie."

At this, Ken went inside and awakened Winna, while Willa went down to the boat and drew it upon the bank of the stream to get the water out of it which had been splashed in by his hurried dash across the stream.

It was never told us if G. G. ma Winna revealed all the happenings of this eventful day, but as I grew older and learned the later consequences of her life—using my own imaginations I just guessed things myself. However Ken took the big bearskin blanket, as he called it, and placed it in the bottom of the skif and bade Winna sit on it as they rowed her back across the stream to the plantation. When they landed it was about 4:30 A. M. He took the bear skin and wrapped it about Winna and carried her over his shoulder to the cabin. He then patted Willa lightly on the shoulder and whispered, "Mon good friend," and walking over to Winna he looked longingly at her then holding her face between his big brawny hands, bent over and placed a light kiss on her forehead, and on each ear, and then with a bound of a deer he was off and down through the lowgrounds and out of sight.

Dropping the Rug from her shoulders, Winna walked to the little wooden window of her cabin room and gazed out into the twilight of the morning and wondering if Ken was going away forever like the darkness of the fleeting night. She turned to find Willa gone and She, being alone in her cabin room, took up the rug and examined it closely, realizing at the same time that it was more valuable than any thing she had ever had. She spread it on her bed and vowed within her mind that she would keep it and give it to her first little pickaniny that came.

~//~

Chapter 4
Kheenee Sioux Comes to Ask for Winna

FROM THIS TIME on, until their final parting came, Kheenee Sioux was forever begging for Winna. He pleaded with Willa, He asked Winna's two girl friends to appeal to Winna's Master in his behalf. He kept this up day upon days until Winna, who for some reason or other was not so bright and lively as she was in the habit of being, decided that she would take it upon herself to go to her mistress, Since her Master was out of town on political business or some sort of thing pertaining to the work of electing a president for the Nation, and ask her if she could get married.

Well, early one morning in August, as the crops were all ripening and the slaves had, for a couple of weeks, but little to do in the fields, they were all surprised by the sight of an Indian coming slowly but surely up the great lane to the big house, They were all at attention when the Redman came up to the gate and inquired of them for their master. The foremost boy whirled around, trotted to the back and told the houseboy or butler, that an indian was asking for the Master, At the same time, the mistress who was upstairs in her chamber, had also looked out from her window and spied this indian. At first She was of the opinion that possibly he was on his way to the Indian reservation and had lost his way. So she hurried downstairs and sent all the slaves away but the butler and the houseboy which as we know, one of these boys was Willa.

Willa did not let on that he knew the indian. Neither did the indian show any recognition of Willa. Mistress Lucinda Robinson, the Master's Wife, bade the indian to come to the porch and sit down. Which he did very reverently.

"Now," said she, "Can I be of any service to you?"

"Yes," said the Indian, bowing very low. "Me am Kheenee Sioux, Me wishes to ask her Master and mistress as to let me have Winna for myself, please." Mistress Lucinda grew frantic with disgust.

"Let you have what?" She snapped at him.

"Winna, Winna, your slave girl. me want her please for um wigwam."

"What do you know about Winna?" she asked.

"Me see her many times at um big stream fishing."

"Did Winna tell you that she wanted you?"

"No, no," blurted out the Indian, "She just say Massa will kill me."

"Do you know that Indians and negroes are not allowed to live together?" asked Mrs. Robinson.

"Me alone," said Ken, "me got no mammy no pappy, nothing but me wigwam."

"Well," said Mrs. Robinson, "No, you can't have Winna nor any other slave girl on this plantation. So don't be caught on it again if you value your life. Be gone now and don't bother any more."

With this the Indian bowed and left with the two boys who escorted him outside of the gate. It is needless to relate that Willa told Winna all that was done and said.

~//~

Chapter 5
The Mistress Has a Talk with Winna

AFTER THIS EVENTFUL day described above, all was forgotten concerning our G. Grandma and the Indian, seemingly until one day right out of a blue sky Mrs. Robinson sent to have Winna brought to her in her bedchamber. Winna, who at this time was beginning to get used to her natural condition, combed her hair, bathed and put on a clean, homespun dress and went upstairs to her mistress' bedroom. She stood at the door with her hands locked together in front of her and her head bowed.

"Come in Winna," ordered Mrs. Robinson, "and sit down here on this foot stool."

"Yessum Missis" trembled Winna.

Mrs. Robinson was reading a book which seemed to interest her intensely. She did not say anymore to Winna for more than twenty minutes. Then laying her book down, She looked at Winna and, seemingly, with eyes of pity she looked away for a while. Then with a slight chuckle of annoyance She began with:-

"Well Winna I am quite sure you know what I wish to see you about."

Winna sat gazing at the floor, but said nothing.

"Are you deaf Winna?" She asked disgustingly.

"Nom missus" trembled Winna.

"Then why don't you answer me?" She snapped.

"Ah don know what Missus wan me to say" whined Winna tremolously.

"What have you done with that Indian? You Vile Villian!" said Mrs. Robinson abusively.

"Ah don nuffin wid im Missus."

"Don't lie to me Winna I will have all of your black hide blistered if you do. And I shall have your Master sell you down to Missippi before you have his whole plantation run over by Indians. Didn't you know better that to have anything to do with indians? I had so much confidence in you Winna, and you have destroyed it all. You are really no more service to me, and when your Master comes home I shall have you sold far, far away."

At this assertion, Winna fell at her mistress' feet shaking most excessively with weeping and imploring,

"Please missus don send me from mah poh brudder."

"Where is Willa?" asked Mrs. R. speaking now a little calmer.

"He dun been bout de cook room" sniffled Winna. She called one of the housemaids and had Willa brought in.

Willa stood at the door until she bad him come in. He came in and stood just as Winna had done.

"Willa," she asked "What do you know about this Indian?"

"De fust tarm ah seed him was when we went to de holerdy fishing. and Wina she fell in de big stream and dis man he dun cum from out de tree un jump in de watah un fetch er out. Yesum Missy, den afer he wuz so kine to hur we wuz glad, un den we tawk to him. but Missus we clar we diden no he wuz a injun, we jes thought he wuz a man."

At this admission Mrs. R. hurriedly got up from her chair and turned her back to Winna and Willa, pretending to be looking out of the window. But in truth She was hiding her feeling of pity for, what she thought of them as, the poor heathens. facing them again She asked abruptly:

"Willa do you know that Winna is going to give birth to a child?" Willa's eyes widened.

"Nom Missus, dat ah diden. Lawsy! what Massa and Missus gwine do to my poh sissie! I don know."

"Shut up," said Mrs. R. "You know what I ought to do. I should sell her a way down in Missippi where she will be whipped every day until that child is born."

"Oh, please missus if you don sell poh Winna I'll look for dat injun and kill him sho he bon."

"Well get out now and don't give us any more trouble mixing with free niggers and indians, or we will sell you both. You sit there on that stool Winna untill I tell you to go," said she ironically and left the room. It was way after supper when she came again to the room and found Winna sitting there on the stool a veritable object of pain and fear. She felt as though she had grown to the stool.

"Alright Winna you are to sleep in the big clothes closet to my sister's room until your Master come. I have had Ellen fix you a pallet in there that you may sleep on. You must not go any more to the kitchen untill you get new orders. I shall have you in here to knit or hemstitch if I need to. Get up now and go to your bed and don't come out again tonight."

This, Winna was very glad to do, and from which she really rested fast asleep till morning.

~//~

Chapter 6
Back to Kheenee Sioux

LET US NOT forget the day that Mrs. R. had given the Indian the strict orders to stay away from the plantation. Nevertheless, the Indian never gave up hope of getting Winna. But, obedient to her command to leave the place, he made his way from the great house. It being the time of year when, even as it seemed the forest with beast and flying insects of the various kinds, were all resting from a spell of labour they were scampering to and fro, here and there through the leafy mead as Ken, walking as lazily as his meadow companions, drifted, deep in thought, along the narrow footpath made only by him and the wild forest beasts. Not in all his life had Ken felt so all alone before. Arriving at the stream, he went about to unloose his skiff, when lo, he observed a shaking of movement of the branches of a clump of shrubbery. Grasping his sling, he squatted close to the ground, keeping a tense gaze on the shrubbery, as if to take into survey, every leaf and line therein, when, through the hot still atmosphere, came a tremolous soft voice, "Kheenee Sioux;" Like a tiger springing on his prey, Ken sprang at the bush, grabbing the owner of the voice, shrubbery and all, in his joyfull excitement, he was, not realizing it, holding his object so tight and close, that it was almost painful.

"Oh, Winna! Winna," he fairly moaned, "What angel brought my Winna?" Winna loosed his hold, enough to get her breath. Then she placed her hands over his mouth and softly said, "Hush Khee-nee. I must say sumpin quick and fast. I is sorry, un I is glad too, dat you ask Missus bout me, but please, please, Ken don't come to de house no mo caus Missus done swar she gon to sell me down Missippi way un den I cain cum fo to see you no mo. Please Ken tell me you wan cum no mo caus I kin cum sum tahm to see you. Promise me quick fo sum nigger ketch me heah." The Indian pulled Winna's head to his breast and chanted in his own language, something that Winna did not understand, but she always remembered the melody. Ken raised Winna's face to his and whispered, "Poor helpless slave, you shall be free. I have two bags of um gold of white man, I will buy you from dem." At this point there came over the air a long baying sound of a dog. "Go Ken! Go Ken!" shrieked Winna, "de lead bloodhound is cummin."

"No, no," shouted Ken, "I killum bloodhound."

"Den," moaned Winna, "Massa kill Winna." At this assertion he gave Winna a deep warm embrace and slid off the banks of the stream into his skiff and across the stream he headed. Winna turned to run back through the low grounds in order to escape the bloodhound, which fortunate for her Willa was down there gathering weeds for the calves and hogs. He gave her the small bag and he took the heavier and said,

"Now don run no mo: I saw you when you started down heah and I don grab two bags un follow you." At this time Winna was put at her ease and went back to the house safe, only to find the message from her Mistress to come to her.

Soon, it became known that Winna was taken from the kitchen, and also for what reason she was taken. Many questions were asked of the assistant cooks, who of course were Winna's only associates, but the girls (Lena and Jane) stayed mum to all the questioning as they and Willa, and Winna were devoted friends.

It was not for punishment that Mrs. R. took Winna from the kitchen to the chambers. But knowing that Winna was approaching motherhood, she felt that it would be easier on her if she did sewing and knitting instead of being on her feet all day in the kitchen. She used to send her to the kitchen to give the main instructions when she had company in for dinner. We note here that G. Grandma's owners were as devoted to their slaves as they were to the rest of the family, that is as far as being in a slaves place was concerned.

Winna took hold on to her new environment and new duties with a willing and humble spirit. When at last the weeks of leisure for the farm and field workers was at an end, and everything began astir, Winna gathered together the different pieces of work which she had done since she was in the great house. So many pairs of socks, so many pairs of gloves, so many pairs of stockings, and even had done the hemstitching for one of her Mistress' wide petticoats. The work pleased Mrs. R. Very much. So when it came to harvest time She gave Winna permission for the first time in four months, to go out with the plantation slaves to a corn shucking party given by a group of slaves of another plantation owner. Willa was wild with joy when Winna came over to the cabin and told him the good news. He made her comfortable by the cabin fire, and reached up over the door and took down his bow and arrow, which he and Ken had fashioned for him, and said to his sissie, "Ah is goin ovah to de next plantation an fix a seat at de con pile for you to set tonite sis, you stay heah tel I gits back." But did Willa go to fix the seat at the corn pile? No. He made a beeline to Ken's wigwam. Kheenee made a whoop which gave Willa the shivers.

"Hey, d-d-don make too loud," sputtered Willa, "dem bloodhounds de come fo us. I is heah to git fum you whar you want me to bring Winna to fust, heah or at de con pile?"

"Make me no diffrence," laughed the Indian, "me mity glad to see my good squaw love."

"Who be dat?" queried Willa.

"That's me Winna, me poor Wina," poured forth the Indian. "Willa, mon, fetch her to Kheenee and I give you big skin for cap." Willa mad a leap and a bound and he was in the skiff back across the stream. It was good and dark when he immerged from the edge of the forest, so he got back to the cabin unnoticed.

"Did you find a seat Willa?" asked Winna.

"You bet I did," Will assured her.

Lena and Jane came over and combed and fixed Winna's hair, enveloping it in a beautiful net which Winna had knitted before she left the kitchen. They helped her get dressed, because Winna at this late date was a little deficient in turning about too fast. Lena and Jane had dates to go with them to the corn shucking, so Willa went with Winna. Coming to the edge of the forest, Winna asked Willa curiously, "Is dis de way to de shucking boy?"

"Dis is de way to de shucking dat I is carin you," chuckled Willa.

"Ah don no what you mene," said Winna looking about furtively.

"Ah mene ah is gwinter bring you fust to Ken, un den ah is gwinter bring you to de con shucking arter."

"Oh Willa," said Winna, "Ah is feeling truble when you say dat caus Missus mout find out un sell we."

"Let er sell we den," growled Willa, "caus she is lookin fur Marsus de nite and I no he can't sell we cause we b'long to Miss Harriet Smith un she is way up Norf way. I hear um say when I was in de chamber las nite."

"Yeah?"

"Yeah," said Willa. "an moun dat, Ken dun beg fer you, and he is offern gold fer you what mo do dey want." Of course Willa had the thought of that nice coon skin cap that Ken had promised him too.

"Well," said Winna, somewhat deep in thought, "Ah tol Ken don cum heah no mo so ah guess ah haf to go to heme, but missus will sho gie me sumpin bad to do."

"Wal," said Willa, "Don you wan to see Ken?"

"Oh! Yes sho!" exclaimed Winna, "Mo dan eny sumpin mo in dis land, I want to see my Ken and" just when she had opened her mouth to say another word it was muffled by a big hand which spread even across her cheeks, and at the same time Ken was holding Winna with the other arm, just ejaculating something in his own language and touching his emblem that he carried around his neck. He then held her off at arms length and looked at her and grinned. Winna was so elated she just looked at Ken and big tears rolled down her tawny cheeks.

"How you been, My Wenna!?" asked Ken sympatheticly.

"Ah is been in de great house ebery since I seen you las, Ken," smiled Winna through her tears which was as the sun shining through showers. Willa, who could never stand to see his sis shed tears even if they were tears of joy, made ready to go off.

"Wal," said he, "Ah is going over to de udder plantation ovah heah un see if dey dun started to shuck corn. un if dey done started, ah kin stay tell ah gits one or two piles dun fo I cum back can't ah?" Winna made the move to start with Willa at which Ken caught her gently and grinned assuringly, telling her that he must see her a little more, and if she would please remain with him until Willa came back. Of course he and Willa had made their plans before Winna was brought down.

"Wal den," said Winna, "Ah stay, don be too long." Willa was off with a bound because he was one of the group which made the music for the dance and he had to do so many piles of corn before he stopped.

The evening being damp with dew, Ken persuaded Winna, who was now a little tired after coming all through the low-grounds with Willa, to go across to the wigwam with him, and rest while they waited for Willa. Winna agreed to go, as she thought to herself that since Missus knew that they had gone to a corn shucking which always lasted through the night, she would not be looking for her back before day.

As they rowed off from the bank of the stream, Winna looked up at Ken's face, and rejoiced inward to see the expression of joy and delight at having her with him. Having reached the other side he helped her out and brought her to the wigwam which was so inviting and cheerful inside. He quickly pulled out his jug of brandy and poured Winna a good bit in a gourd which he took from hanging by the door. She sipped it as she looked around in the wigwam, and thought of the indescribable pleasure she had experienced when she was here last. She forgot everything else; even the day she sat for six hours on a stool without even moving up from it. All this was forgotten as she remembered her pleasure here with Ken.

Ken's cot, which was always kempt and clean looked so inviting that Winna took the privilege to rest on it, before being told to do so by Ken. Now nothing was more elating to Ken, when, coming in with a dried squirrel which he had hung on a pole outside, to find Winna resting on his cot. After playing and teasing with her for a while, he prepared a most delectable Indian supper of dried broiled squirrel, roasted corn cob, and hot sassafras tea and parched corn cake with butter. Winna was ashamed of herself at how much she ate but Ken was overjoyed at the whole affair.

After supper, she lay, still, on the couch while they swapped time, telling the experience of their lives, until Winna fell asleep. She slept more than three hours, and during the time, Ken searched among his belongings to see what he could find which could be of any service to his Winna. Among the things chosen were, one leather jacket, two pairs of moccasins which he himself had fashioned, two wampums which were his mother's and a big piece of raw gold that he had taken from his daddy's neck when he got killed by the white raiders. All these he kissed and chanted over softly and did a quiet dance so as not to awaken Winna. He placed them in a nicely cleaned and finished case of the skin of some animal, and tied them up, ready for Winna when Willa should come. As he sat and peered out into the night, there came over the air the clear whistle so well known now to Ken. He jumped up and ran down to the stream and called back, standing there until Willa got over. He pulled Willa in who was quite high, now, with posimmon beer.

"Whar is Winna?" he asked casually.

"She is at the Wigwam sleep," said Ken looking enquiringly at Willa. "What! You happy Willa?" asked Ken.

"No, no, ah is dry," croaked Willa, as he pulled from his hip pocket a flask and turned it up to drink more.

"No, no, you must not," said Ken, taking the flask, "How you take Winna home?"

"Ah take hur; don you git so funny," said Willa, "or I go back un leave hur here."

"Now don't speak like so my friend," pleaded Ken, "You will make Winna sad and fearful."

"Wal, bring hur heah den un I take hur to de shucking."

Kheenee Sioux went back to the wigwam for Winna and when he went in, she was up and looking at the things about the Wigwam.

"Hey Ken, whar you bin?" she asked. "I bin looking for you in de yard."

"Willa called me, and I went to him," Ken spoke looking somewhat bewildered. Seeing how blank and void his countenance was, Winna came to him quickly, taking hold of his shoulders, "What is it, Ken? You look skert and sorry what is dun now?"

Taking Winna fully in his embrace he touched her forehead with his lips uneasily and looking about him, he began.

"Winna, my only one, I will tell you someting. Your brother is mity happy with fruit jack. Here is the other I took from him. He no can take you home tonight. I fetch him here til he is no more happy. I take you to your cabin while everyone is away with the corn husking."

"Oh, oh! Ken, dere is gonna be trouble for us all, dey will ketch you and kill you. Jes bring me to the edge of de low ground an ah will find de way home."

"No, Winna, I will not let you out alone. I will bring Willa and leave him here while I take you home. Trust me will you, Winna? I promise I will fix all things good."

"Ah wait den," said Winna confidentially.

Hurriedly Ken went back to the stream, aroused Willa who was by now almost out and veritably dragged him back to the wigwam. When Winna saw Willa she started to cry, but Ken assured her that he was only happy from too much posimmon beer. He put him upon the cot. He thought about the sack he had fixed to carry with Winna.

"Oh," said he, "I have something for you, and too, I have a little gift for our new papoose." Saying this, he took from over the top of the door a little sack made like an all over garment for an infant, only this was made from the fine skin of a young moose.

"What is this be, Ken?" Winna asked as she held it up proudly.

"It be to carry um papoose in," he said grinning broadly and rubbing Winna's hair at the same time.

"Thank you," she said and stuffed it in the sack with the other things, and they put out on their journey.

As they rowed toward the other bank of the stream Winna ventured to tell Ken that her master was due home tonight and she was so scared, wondering what her mistress was going to tell him.

"Tell him I will buy you Winna and give him two bags of white man's gold for you. Then he can buy other women who I do not want." But Winna answered him that her master valued her very highly because he had had her trained from a little girl to sew, knit, and do all kinds of cooking, and that she was depended upon to train the assistant help.

"Moun' dat," said Winna, "dey don want dat de slaves be wit de red folk so dey mout kill you if you come to de plantation, and I don wan dat to happen."

On arriving at the bank of the stream Ken helped Winna on shore, made his skiff more secure and started off through the forest with Winna holding fast to his arm. He made the shortest cut to Winna's cabin. On reaching it he said nothing, he just held her very secure for a split moment, then embraced her fondly and turned away swiftly and was gone.

Winna took her precious gifts from Ken and opened her Mammy's old chest and put everything in it without looking at them, as she was anxious to get into the big house before the doors were locked downstairs. After she changed her clothes, old aunt Lena came out and asked her, "have yo see Mars George, Winna?"

"No, whar he be?" asked Winna.

"Come heah," called old aunt Lena. She pointed to the big long parlor window.

"Yo see dem dere? Dey is tawkin about niggers. yo bettah git to yo pallet fo dey git at you. Ah is takin kere of yo, ah don go no whar hunny, ah jes stay heah."

"Thank you, Aint Lena," says Winna, and she stole in quietly to her pallet in the big closet.

~//~

Chapter 7
Listening into Pandora's Box

WINNA HAD BEEN in bed about ½ hour when she heard voices and knew that they were her Master and mistress coming upstairs to the bedchamber. She feigned sleep, while she listened with intense anxiety to what they said.

Mr. R. When are you expecting your sister, Pat?

Mrs. R. I don't know Dear, she didn't say anything about coming when I heard from her last.

Mr. R. Are you going to redecorate the house before she comes back?

Mrs. R. Well, that depends on the success of the farm. You know how much money will be spent going to the Leadbetter's Ball. I will have to buy everything new, and you will need a new suit, if you can order it and get it from France in time.

Mr. R. Oh pshaw, dear I don't need anything new. I will wear the suit that I took office in last fall. I have not worn it but once since then.

Mrs. R. Oh yes, George you must get a suit of the latest style, even if you have to sell a slave.

Mr. R. Never, Dear, never! I haven't enough slave labor as it is, and I surely will not sell one. The fact is I hope to be able to buy two or more slaves this Winter.

Mrs. R. Well, under these circumstances there will be no chance of getting the house decorated. Oh, George dear, I didn't tell you what has happened to Winna our head cook?

Mr. R. What, is she dead?

Mrs. R. Oh, pshaw dear don't be silly. No, she is not dead; she is quite alive. She is going to have a baby.

Mr. R. Ah ha! that will mean one more slave without having to buy it.

Mrs. R. But George you have not the slightest idea who she is having the child by.

Mr. R. Whom, by a free nigger?

Mrs. R. No, no, George, Mrs. R. said impatiently. It's by an Indian.

Mr. R. What! turning to his wife. Where did she get in touch with an Indian?

Mrs. R. I do not know dear, I hear from Willa, that they met last spring somehow, when Winna, by accident, fell into the big branch where they were fishing. It seems that this Indian dived in and saved Winna's life, and that was the introduction which led to this negro and Indian romance, and as you know, the slaves and Indians are not allowed to be found together.

Mr. R. Did any of the other slaves know of this?

Mrs. R. No, I don't think so, only her brother Willa and he swore to me that they did not know he was an indian, they thought only that he was a red man.

Mr. R. Ha ha ha: you know, I guess they didn't know any different poor fools.

Mrs. R. Well dear don't you think Winna should be punished for becoming intimate with a stranger like that?

Mr. R. I don't know; I think its enough punishment, on her part, to have to have a baby, don't you, darling?

Mrs. R. Well, suppose she is taken away by the Indian?

Mr. R. Oh, I don't think she would leave the plantation. In fact, I don't think he would want her with him and, according to all law, the child will be ours.

Mrs. R. Yes dear, he will want her if he can get her, he has already said it , in so many words to me.

Mr. R. To you; where did you see him?

Mrs. R. He came here to our front gate and asked permission to see the master. I came out to the porch and offered my assistance if I could be of any help. I thought, maybe, he had lost his way to some reservation, and wished information about the way to go. But when he informed me that he wished that the good master let him have Winna for himself, I was dumbfounded. I ordered him off the plantation and ordered him never to come here again, under a penalty of getting shot.

Mr. R. Ah ha, have you had any more trouble since then?

Mrs. R. No, but I don't know if he has been around or not. Of course I made Winna come in here a few days after that, and I have kept her here every since, until tonight, I let her go out to a corn husking party over to the Bendicks plantation.

Mr. R. Well, my dear, do you think that was necessary? She is only a slave, and this is her first child is it not? And you know Pat, Winna is reaching way up in age she is nearly forty isn't She?

Mrs. R. Yes, but that is no excuse for her to go straying out after an Indian, as many negro slaves as it is about: and another thing, it may start trouble with the tribes.

Mr. R. Oh no dear: there are some Indian negroes on almost every plantation in Virginia. Anyway I will talk with Winna tomorrow, or sometime before I go away again. To whom do Winna and Willa belong, to you or Harriet?

Mrs. R. They belong to our estate equally. I told Winna I was going to sell her.

Mr. R. Well that you can't do without Harriet's signature can you? And that will have to be ratified by the bank which handles the Smith's estate, since Harriet is not of age yet.

Mrs. R. Oh well, I told her that anyway. So that she may behave hereafter.

Mr. R. You know dear it may be that we can catch that Red and hold him as a hostage for enough skins to cover all our hunting saddles and to make all the bridles and line that is needed on the place.

Mrs. R. Yes, but who will you hold him against?

Mr. R. That's right too. Well I do hope you send Winna to the kitchen tomorrow, as I am expecting my hunting group tomorrow to be hunting through the forest all day and we will need a plenty of food when we come in, and I want it done right.

Mrs. R. All right dear I will call her and tell her when she comes in, that is if I am not asleep.

~ / / ~

Chapter 8
In Diversion & The Huntsmen

OF COURSE WINNA could not have gotten a better amount of information concerning how her mistress and master felt about her case, if she herself had been present with them: she lay there and took in every word and gesture, from beginning to end. And when they had done with talking She turned up on her knees and elbows, and for the first time in her life, repeated to herself the words which she had heard Aunt Leana say so many times, that she knew them by heart as, "Lawd I do thank you for dese blessings" and for some reason, Winna knew not why, there came over her a strange new feeling of peace and joy. She stretched out on her pallet and went to sleep like an innocent babe in her Mistress' big empty clothes closet.

The next morning, by Sunup, the yard was full of horses, hounds and huntsmen. All ready for a days run. From the forest, at close of day there were brought many a deer. Among the huntsmen was Mrs. Robinson's brother Ned Smith, a man of about 25–30 years. Winna had directed and had prepared to serve a magnificent dinner. The big dining table was open to its greatest length and breadth. All candles were lighted, and dining servants with their caps and aprons, and clean bare feet were all about. Some standing at their posts at the table fanning off flies and skeeters and others filling water glasses, while another group were busy placing the first course of the meal on the table. The huntsmen were in the den, just off the dining room, indulging in appetisers of various kinds. While in the middle course of the meal the discussion of the Indians was begun. They talked on different tribes and how they thought that the Indians were at this time, very well subdued. At this point Mr. R. sprung up exclaiming, "Say gentlemen! The Indians are parked nearer to us than you think. One has been romancing with my head cook while I was away, so I am told: he even got so brazen as to come here to the house to beg for her hand in marriage! At which they all laughed merrily. It's no joke, Its real gospel," chuckled Mr. R. Ned Smith, Mrs. R.'s Brother, sat his glass down with a thump!

"Say, George, you don't really mean that do you?" he asked with a look of a tiger ready for attack.

"Yes," answered Mr. R. "I think he must belong to the Reservations from way up by the Ohio, or he may be just tramping along the banks of the Nottaway River."

"Well what do you say!" warbled Mr. Ned Smith, "Boys," he began, "Let's go up these banks of the forest tomorrow and catch him and hang him by his neck? Why the Red Villian; to get the nerve to come to this plantation to ask for one of the slave wenches for a wife; who will go with me tomorrow to hunt him out of our forest?" At which time five or six volunteered to go with him.

"I will fix the hangman's noose before I sleep tonight," he vowed as he quaffed copiously of his rum.

~//~

Chapter 9
The Grapevine Telegraph

IT IS ALMOST needless to say, that from the time that Winna's name was called in the dining room, every servant who was serving dinner cocked their ears and alerted their senses that they may hear and understand every thing that was said. And if ever they, in serving, passed close enough one to the other they rub elbows hard enough together to give the sign, "catch all you can." Therefore when the dinner was over and everything put in place those same servants all got together and paid a special visit to Willa's cabin. What resolution was adopted was not written but all orders were strictly carried out to the last bidding. The result was, that the next morning all servants were at their posts of duty, but what with the whole plantation agoing, there was missing one of the huntsmen horses saddle and all.

The horn that summoned every slave on the plantation was blown and every one was found in place, but no one knew anything about the missing steed. Mr. R., with two or three of the huntsmen rode to the adjoining plantations to inquire of a stray horse was among their herd, but none was found. Mr. R. was very much outdone that such a thing should occur like this to one of his visiting friends; but what could be done to remedy the inconvenience of his guest was the problem now.

As they stood together in the yard talking and trying to reason or come upon some reasonable plan to lead to the missing horse, all at once Mrs. R.'s brother jumped on a plan. Popping his fingers excitedly, he came up to the group.

"Boys," he began, "I bet a horse I know where the horse is!"

"Where, where!?" They all cried.

"He ain't no place but somewhere in that Indian's possession. I know what I am talking about. Those Indians will steal money from a dead man's pocket if given just half a chance. Mount the horses, men, and let's go through the valley that joins us here. If we do catch that red, his goose and his jackass both will be cooked." With this assertion, all the huntsmen mounted their horses and galloped away to the forest. All the slaves went about their several duties, just as if nothing had happened.

~//~

Chapter 10
A Discovery

THE HUNTSMEN HAD gone quite some distance in the forest when they came upon the big stream. They drew up to a stop. While pondering what to do, the leader of the bloodhounds came up sniffing with his nose almost plowing a furrow as he moved along. As he got near to the group he gave out a deep urgent moan; and into the stream he plunged, the other hounds following. The huntsmen stood attentively watching until the hounds swam across and lighted up the woods with their cries.

"Come on, boys," shouted Mr. S. as he drove his horse down into the stream. In a jiffy all horses, with their riders tugging on to the saddles were soon across and, on a long stretch following the hounds. When they came up to the hounds, which were all in a huddle at an old torn down Indian wigwam, they dismounted to make an inspection of the place They found that the Wigwam had been freshly torn apart. They found in the yard a sack of stone arrows but no bow. They noticed that there were fresh tracks about the place but they could not make out if they were tracks of animals or of men. As they were about to mount their horses, Mr. Ned S. spied, laying by a post of the Wigwam, a pin checked head kerchief with the letter "R" in the corner of it.

"Hey, what's this?" he asked, coming over to Mr. R. Taking the kerchief and looking it over, he said,

"I have seen something like this before, but I just can't remember where."

"What's that letter 'R.' mean there in the corner?" said he, pointing to the letter.

"Oh!" exclaimed Mr. R. "This must belong to some of the slaves, and if it does, we have a wonderful clue to the horse thief."

"I told you," exclaimed Mr. S. excitedly, "that the Indian was the thief, and you can see by this, that he had some help from a slave."

Every one quickly mounted and galloped back to the house, taking with them the arrows and the head kerchief.

Arriving at the house they dismounted and being so excited, they hardly noticed the stable men who was standing ready to care for their horses.

They all gathered in the drawing room and summoned Mrs. R.

"Looka here, Sis," said Mr. S. calling to Mrs. R. "Do you recognize this thing I have here?"

Mrs. R. took hold one corner of the kerchief and then loosed it.

"Yes," said She. "It belong to one of the house servants; where did you get it?"

"Ah," chuckled Mr. Ned Smith, "You don't keep correct watch on the slaves. They are carting off the whole plantation to the Indians, even the guests' horses."

"What are you talking about, Ned?" asked Mrs. R., disgustingly.

"Call the house winches to the back porch and you will find out what I am talking about."

"That I will not do until after dinner," declared Mrs. R. sarcastically, "so please gentlemen, get washed and prepared for dinner." In the meantime She ordered the servants to set the table and serve the dinner, while She tidy up and get ready. Of course, we need not wonder if the grapevine was alert, because we are quite certain that it was. Therefore it was soon made known among the house servants that a cap was found at the freshly torn down Indian wigwam which must belong to one of the house servants. This put every servant to looking for their kerchief. Every one had theirs but Jane.

"Oh Lawsy Laws," shrieked Jane, "Ah am gwine to be kilt Lawsy! What am ah gwine to do?" Winna came from the kitchen and placed her cap on Jane's head.

"Stop yo fussin' gal fo' de white folks heah you. Heah is yo' head rag."

"What yo' gwina do, Winna? Dey gwine sell yo'."

"What ah gwine keah fo'? Ken is gon fer evah," said Winna tearfully. "Now don nobody no nuffin, ah is de ony one wen to de wigwam." This arrangement having been made, the grapevine rested from their uneasiness.

~//~

Chapter 11
Winna's Trial and Punishment

AFTER DINNER, THE horn which summoned the house maids was blown, and every maid from the kitchen to the parlor came to the back porch. Mr. Ned Smith, Mrs. Robinson's brother, came to the edge of the porch and asked, "To whom does this kerchief belong?"

Winna came forth with her head bowed and knelt on the steps at his feet and humbly said,

"Hit belong ter me, marsa." At which he lashed out with it striking her across the face.

"There she is, Patsy," he sneered, "the dirty thieving culprit. Come here you," he demanded of one of the maids by pointing to her, "go into the harness shed and bring me one of those horse whips." Winna was still kneeling on the step not even looking up.

"What are you going to do, Ned?" asked Mrs. R.

"I am going to lash her until she tells me why was her headpiece at that Indian's wig."

"Well I think you should leave that for me to try first." said Mrs. R., who as by now very much annoyed over the whole affair.

"Come here Ned, I wish to speak with you alone," she sharply requested. As they entered the hall She turned on her brother furiously,

"I am not going to allow you to whip that slave Ned, she has never been whipped by anyone but her mother and I am not going to have you whipping her, especially now. She might get excited and lose the child, and for nothing."

"Oh," put in Mr. S., "I am just going to scare her, I am not for pelting her, Pat. She needs a little frightening for ever having anything to do with an Indian."

"Very well then," said Mrs. R. as her brother came out, and she went to the drawing room to take her afternoon nap.

"All you winches go about your work," he commanded, sending all the servants but Winna, away. Mr. R. had already invited the huntsmen for a smoke and drink. Reaching down he grabbed hold of Winna's hair and pulled her jerkingly, to the shed by the barn. He strapped her wrists and tied her hands to a post.

"Now," said he, "what was your head kerchief doing at that Indian's wigwam, Nigger?"

"Ah don know Massa." whimpered Winna.

"Don't start lying to me, you villain or I will blister your black hide from head to feet," he growled with the scowl of an angry beast. "Where did that Indian savage go?"

"Ah don know Marsa." With a stunning blow he lashed into Winna causing her to swing to and fro pulling hard against her fettered wrists.

"Tell me," he muttered savagely, "who stole your master's horse?"

"Ah don noe Marsa," moaned Winna All this horrible barbarity was being secretly witnessed by one of the stable men, who, when he saw the skin on Winna's wrist were torn by the wringing and twisting of the body, could not stand to see it any longer, without venturing to get help. Running over to Willa's cabin, he found him just going out to the big house.

"Uh, Willa!" he whispered excitedly, "Mars Ned is killing Winna! Run tell Missus, boy! Run!" Willa made a bound for the house as if it was on fire. When his foot hit the first step to the porch he let out a cry,

"Lawsy, Missus! Lawsy! Lawsy!" All the house servants, with Mrs. R. came running to the back porch.

"What on earth is going on?" demanded Mrs. R. Willa fell face down at Mrs. R.'s feet.

"Please um Missus!" he cried shaking with emotions. "Mah po sissie is gitten whupped de deth don at de bahn," [getting whipped to death down at the barn.] screamed Willa, wildly.

"Shut up Willa!" demanded Mrs. R. impatiently. "Come with me to the barn." She ordered, Willa was so upset he started off to the barn with a dash way ahead of Mrs. R.

"Come back here Willa," She called out to Willa, "and wait for me." Willa slowed up a bit as he shook with rage and grief, to think that his poor sister was being so heinously punished.

As Mrs. R. came up on Winna and her brother, he was lashing away savagely on Winna cursing out oaths that he will kill her if she didn't tell what she knew.

"You will do nothing of the sort!" almost snorted Mrs. R. "Go there Willa," she ordered. "Take those lines from Winna's wrists." Then turning angrily to her brother, she asked angrily, "Is this what you mean to be just frightening? I think it is more like murder."

"I ... I ... was—er just trying to get her to tell me if she knew who took the horse," he stammered, almost breathless.

"Well," scoffed Mrs. R., "from now on I shall never trust you again with any of my slaves. You have almost ruined this woman. If I had to sell her I could only get half price for her."

"Say Patsy, don't be upbraiding me about lashing a slave. What do you think I am, a hired poor white?"

"All I am asking is that you never whip another slave of mine. I don't whip them myself." And with this she turned and left her brother standing there feeling much put out. She followed the men who took Winna to her cabin and went in to examine the seriousness of Winna's wounds. Winna lay on the couchbed almost completely put out.

"Get some water, wash those wounds off and come to the house. I will give you some rags to bind them with," she [Mrs. R.] said to Lenna as she left the cabin. It was some three or four weeks before Winna could be of any service in the kitchen, but she bore her bruises patiently. She knew as she lay there sometime writhing with the pain of her bruised wrists, that Ken was somewhere in the land, free and alive. With these pleasant thoughts she fell asleep in her little cabin room with her head pillowed upon the precious skins which Ken had placed in the skiff the day before, just before he mounted a horse at dawn leaving his dismantled Wigwam behind forever.*

*We note here that the raw gold that Ken gave Winna was never knowingly made use of. Maybe Winna carried it back to Ken and he took it on his getaway.

As time passed, the preceding events were to a certain extent forgotten. The waning autumn was giving way for the winter. All crops were garnered and put in places prepared for them. Christmas and New Year holidays were in the bygone days and plans for a future crop were being made.

It was at this season of the year on the thirtieth of January, 1793 in the early dawn of the morning that Winna was awakened to the testing and duties of motherhood, assisted by Aunt Lenna and the plantation midwife. And so, was ushered into the world a little Indian-Negro boy who was to be the dearest and best father and grandfather born. [Alexander Sioux Robinson]

The parlor maid told Mrs. R. later in the day of Winna's blessed event. Mrs. R. went to the cabin a week later and recorded the birth of the baby boy, and had planned to name him George Alexander, but Winna begged to have him named Kheenee Sioux.

"Why," says Mrs. R., "that is distinctly an Indian name, Winna and I don't care to have a slave with an Indian tribe name. But," she said meditatively, "anyway I would like to call him first, Alexander. That was my grandfather's name. You may give him any name you like as a second name."

"Please, Missus, let me say Sioux, (pronounced Soo)," pleaded Winna.

"Very well, he shall be called Alexander Sioux," replied Mrs. Robinson. She then took his recorded birth and put it on the slave register. And the child grew and was very alert, wise and industrious having many Indian traits by birth and blood, and was taught many more by his Uncle Willa who was the attentive student of Alexander's father for many moons.

~ / / ~

Chapter 12
Grandfather—"Big Ellec"—Alexander Sioux Robinson

HAVING LOST KHEENEE Sioux, Winna never became interested in any other man. All her time and interest as a mother and sister was centered in her boy and brother the rest of her life. She gave up the duty of cooking, and by permission of her Mistress she learned and practised the duties of a Midwife, which kept her busy most of the time until she was too old for service. She spent much of her leisure reminiscing her short but exultant love affairs. Time and time again, after Ellic was about twelve, she would sit by her cabin fire and confidentially tell him many stories of his father and herself. And often, by Uncle Willa, was he schooled about his dad and their many trips together through the forest along the big river stream. Willa spent most of his leisure time tramping with Alexander over that part of the forest which was the home, and roaming, and hunting, and fishing grounds of Ellic's father, Kheenee Sioux. So much so that Ellic could go all over the route and come home as he felt like it. He had gone quite a few times to the cabins which were rented to the free Negroes and poor whites. It was through the gossip and tales of these groups that he learned, so to speak, quite a little of the outside world. He was a wonderful marksman and had killed, with his dad's own bow and arrow, many heads of game. One morning, just about the dawn of day, in November, he brought down a wonderful specimen of a deer. His master said it was as fine a deer as any pack of hounds and huntsmen could catch. He always kept a supply of pelts of the stoats, ermine, opossum, and seganku ready for sale, for which his young master often traded with him for second hand suits and waistcoats, and often gave him money.

At 14 years of age, my grandfather Alexander had learned almost to perfection, all of the routine arts and duties of the farm. He had learned to follow to the stick, to the end of a row as straight as any experienced plow man on the plantation. He led at the hoe in any race through the field. And I have often heard him say he carried two sets of rows pulling fodder to any man's one set. He also had the honor of out boxing and kicking any grown man who took him to task.

At twenty he was forbidden by law, through his Master, to strike a man with his fist. He could slap a man with whom he did contend or strove, but his fist was considered as an unlawful weapon to his fellow-contenders.

At the age of twenty-one, Granddad Eleck was sent with a large regiment of men to take the place of his young Master, who was, at the time majoring in his school course. During Granddad's enlistment he built many field forts and big bridges in order that the Colonial soldiers could pass over swiftly and safely when they were in combat or in retreat during the war between the U. S. A. and Great Britain in 1813 A. D.

During this war, his Master Ned Smith (who gave Ellec's mother her only whipping) was killed. At Granddad's thirtieth year, he had been overseer over all the field hands. Of course he was not as Legrea [Simon Legree]. My G. Dad was stern but very impartial and never but considerate when it came to judging or adjusting a cause. He did very little strapping to his sheep, but when it was necessary, he had no respect of person. Of course the Robinson Slave owners never allowed poor whites to be overseers to his slaves. Overseers were always chosen from some of the slaves of the plantation. Only once did the owner employ a poor white; and he remained until Granddad was released from the Army, at a time which Granddad took over. He taught and instructed in the art of furrows and the laying off of the grain rows for the planting of the seed and many other arts of the farm.

During this epoch, there was considerable conflict about the problem of slavery and its effect in the country. All these different disputations brought about different squabbles as to what should be done. As I have stated before, Ellec, as Grandad was called for short, use to go often to visit the free Negroes of the neighborhood. And during this period he got hold of quite a big portion of news of the outside world. And, hearing, by the talk of the free Negroes, of the advantage of a man if he is freed and of the disadvantage of being a slave. These things aroused the fighting indian in my Grandad, I am persuaded to believe.

My Grandad Ellic, having met with some of the Agents of the opposers of slavery, joined up with them to go and set the country right. And this is how one morning in the year of 1831 Alexander Sioux, Overseer of the plantation fields of George Chamberlin Robinson was missing from duty. It was five or six months before Big Branch appeared again on the estate.

With many a slave holders there would have been a fresh slave put down in stock. But not so on George C. Robinson's plantation. Although Alexander Sioux was shaking with fear and distress he made his way straight to his master who much to Ellec's astonishment, gave out a great cry of, "hurrah," and exclaimed, "Well! If it ain't Big Branch!" And from that cry of joy came out the Mistress with the rest of the household, slaves and all.

"Where you been Nigger all this time?" He asked jubilantly.

"Marse George ah reckon ah been eberywhar, and den ah reckon ah been nowhar," said Ellec penitently.

"Well what kept you away from here, some D. Yankee Raiders caught you?" asked Mr. R.

"Ah jes got loss an cuden git back. Ah tries all I kud, ah got loss in de dismal swamp an ah done slep wid de bars un de foxes an de snakes, Marsa; am[and] sometime I jes stood all nite in de watah an de mud. Ah dun work all de meat of mah bones tryin to git back heah. Ah is so sorry ah bin gone."

"Well, what caused you to leave?" asked Mr. R., looking around at the rest of the household which stood there.

"Ah wuz dregged way fum heah by dem ole raiders and de didn't tell me whar de wuz gwine," said Ellec, a little sheepishly.

"How do you know it was Dismal Swamp?" asked Mr. R.

"Sum mo niggers sed hit wuz Suh."

"Then you ran away with other Negroes?" questioned Mr. R.

"Naw suh Marser," said Ellic, "ah cum upon a heap o niggers an white mens too what rode on hoses an de made de niggers trot un run on us foots Suh."

"Well, well," said Mr. R., turning to Mrs. R. "Dear," says he, "I bet those raiders belonged to that Nat Turner insurrection. You hear Ellic say he was lost in Dismal Swamp. You know that's where those raiders were overtaken when they retreated." Turning to Ellec he asked excitedly,

"Big Branch did you hear anyone say anything about a man by the name of Nat Turner?"

"No Suh Marser, ah don reckon eber hurin dat name," said Ellec musingly. Of course by now we know just how keen Granddad was, since he answered with the subtlety which made Mr. R. believe he was speaking truthfully yet believing that Ellic was dragged off not knowing that the raiders were a bunch of insurrectors. And from that day to this, Mr. R. never knew any different.

Granddad was placed again as overseer of the field, and all the slaves received him gladly. Maybe somewhere further on in this narrative I shall tell of his experience, when he was away, as he has so many times related it to his mother Winna and to his wife and children and even to his grandchildren. When Winna reached home and found out that Ken had come, (She always called Ellec, Ken) no words can express her joy at seeing him. She always said little Sioux was the image of big Sioux, only big Sioux's hair was straight to the very end, and little Sioux's hair was straight to about two inches of the end and the rest of the length would roll up in a pretty curl which would be the envy of any hair decorator of today. Alexander grabbed his mother up like she was a little girl and spun around the yard with her. When they were seated by the candlelight in the cabin that night, he told his dear ole Mammie everything.

~//~

Chapter 13
1833 A. D.—Courtship and Marriage

HAVING DETERMINED TO settle down now, Ellec stayed close to home, and amused himself more in the neighborhood circles. The plantation slaves gave a Harvest Moon Party one night in November. The dressup worn to this party by Alexander "Ellec" Sioux Robinson was knee breeches of blue home spun thread and a stunningly made red-dyed Indian style coat trimmed around the bottom with yellow scalloped sheepskin. The entire coat was made from the skin of an animal. His uncle Willa had given it to him from his father Kheenee Sioux's chest. The same of which we will speak later on. Winna had been accorded the pleasant privilege of dressing big Sioux's hair for this occasion for which she washed and dried it, then applied some of her new goose grease. Then she parted it in the middle and brushed it down each side to his ears and from there it rolled up in loose curls which just touched his shoulders. The legend goes that Granddad was the most finely dressed beau in the group. Across his chest he wore, for a watch chain, a pair of red and yellow and blue indian made, and dyed, nutberry beads.

When the time for dance began, as the legend goes, the band was made up of mouth harps, the Jew's harp, hand clappers, bones, banjos and drums. Uncle Willa at his best with the ring callers, was put into operation leading with the drum. Also among this group was some of the prettiest young gals to be found from two or three other plantations, and they were of all colors, from black to blank with hair of all grades, from wool to silk. I am told that at such an affair, many of the Masters and Mistresses use to walk around and enjoy watching the Slaves dance and sing. When the band gave the signal and the ring was formed, with men on one side and ladies on the other, the ring caller commenced his calling and the dance was on.

It was during one of the ring calling and choosing on this night, that our boy, Alexander Sioux Robinson, had picked long before his name was called, a bright-eyed cocoanut brown lassie with black shiny hair, combed back and caught with a homespun red net. As he capered and danced up to her at the middle of the ring. He slipped, from across his breast, the string of beads left him by his Dad, and placed them over this girl's head and tied them in a love knot at the throat.

At this the crowd yelled, "Hurrah! Hurrah Big Branch is engaged." The whites who stood on the outside were much amused, and among those whites was a man who, more than any one else, enjoyed the Act.

"Well, I be a chump," says he grinning, "if that ain't my Nigger, Big Branch. He looks almost like a real red man."

When the next dance was set was on, Ellec did not dance. He preferred sitting or standing this dance out, during which time he became more acquainted with his dancing partner.

"Fum what plantation is you?" inquired Big Branch.

"Ah is fum de Bland's plantation," said She.

"What be you name?" said B. B.

"Easter Bland," said She.

"Is you been married?" asked B. B.

"Naw, Suh." answered Easter, somewhat bashful.

"Wal," said B. B., "ah ain't married, and ah like a gal jes like you ef you want to git married."

"Thanky suh, ah is bin thinkin' on de same thang, but who is gwine tell Missus?"

"Ah kin get Mars George ter ask fer me and den if de say yes, I kin cum rite ovaher down, er … up and git you. My Mammy got a nice cabin big enuf for four un us. Ah is cummin an git you termarrah nite and sho you. Which way you come heah?"

"Ah don no, but you cum heah termarrah en mah brudder will bring me heah, an yus kin go to yos mammie's cabin." said Easter.

"Good," said Alexander, as he got up from his seat on the grass. Taking Easter by the hands and assisting her up also.

"Let's dance." said he, and over to the ring they whirled and whirled and then to the middle of the ring where they were lost in the crowd of joy makers.

The next night about ten thirty out at the big threshing field of the combined neighborhood, (This was the place that was always used for the slaves' ballroom.) were two lonely people standing by the fence gap peeping first one way and then another, when much to their ease of mind, though they did wonder, they was a man come bounding over the hill toward them. Easter was almost as breathless from excitement at seeing the runner; as he himself was from running when he came up to them. Sioux, before he greeted them good, had Easter in his arms. But he was brought up to attention by a tug at his sleeve from a little boy about 12 years old and, looking around, the little fellow came up to him and asked pertly,

"Suh, who be yos?" At which Easter laughed, amusingly pleased.

"Oh Sonnie!" grinned Alexander. "Ah be Ellec, yoh sissie's fren. How come yo ax me?"

"Becase," said the lad, "ah jes wanna heah yo say de name wot she tol me." At this information they all laughed and started through the fields to Winna's cabin. Alexander S. Robinson stopped at most all of the slaves' cabins as he went along through the slave grounds, and introduced his Sweetheart to his neighbors. So when he got to Winna's cabin, Easter was no stranger on the plantation.

Ellec had told his mammy what he intended to do this evening so Winna had everything in order. Her floor was scrubbed white and here and there over it, was scattered those beautiful skin rugs of some of the prettiest animals caught by Khee-nee Sioux, Ellec's father.

Easter wore a nice plain homespun cotton dress, her only decoration were the beads which Alexander had placed around her neck the night before. Her hair was arranged the same way as it was the night before. She smiled very broad and happily as she entered the cabin. To cover or conceal the embarrassment in confronting Easter, Winna went right to her and took her into her arms, and exclaimed,

"Oh! Dis is little Miss Easter. Ahm so glad to make your acquaintance. Come right in and be happy you blessed li'l honey gurl." This put Easter quite at her ease. So she and Winna talked and got more acquainted while Ellec went about the plantation to make sure that the slaves had put all their farm implements in place, and that all the team was fed and closed in. When he got back, Winna left them alone while she prepared a small repast. They had just finished eating and had cleared the table when Willa came up and greeted everyone graciously, after which Ellic introduced his Uncle Willa to Easter. So at this point Easter had about met all of Sioux's family and friends. Ellic then accompanied her and her little brother back home, which was about two plantations, or about four miles distance. I am of the opinion that it must have been outside of Brunswick County.

The next morning after Grandad had put the workers out and saw that everything was moving about the plantation, he went to the Servants entrance and sent in word to the Master and Mistress that if they would not be too much troubled he would be pleased for them to let him talk with them about something of importance. When the door boy gave the message to Mr. R., he told him to tell Ellec to stay there on the back porch until he came down.

When Mr. R. came down Ellec was standing holding his hands together in front of him. (He never wore a hat, Winter nor Summer.)

"Well what's so urgent Big Branch?" asked Mr. R.

"Ah don no how to say it Marser, but ah is gwine to ax you to please Suh, ax de plantation Marster on de Bland's farm to gi' me one of his gals what is name Easter fer a wife please Suh."

"Ah ha!" exclaimed Mr. R., with raised brows. "So you are going to make trouble for me now, are you?"

Ellec. No Suh Massa, ah jes think it is time fer me to start me a fambly if you please Suh."

Mr. R. When did you meet this girl, B. B., and what do you know about her?

Ellec. Ah jes seed hur at de harvest ball Suh, and she leck me an ah leck huh Suh, and she dun seed my Mammie Suh.

Mr. R. Well, B. B. I don't see any reason why we should object to you having a wife if you want one. Why don't you take a wife from our plantation?

Ellec. Ah no too much bout dem suh.

At this Mr. laughed and said, "Well allright, B. B., I will talk to your Mistress and we will see what we can do for you."

Ellec. Thankee Suh Marse George, thankee suh.

Mr. R. did not have an easy time getting Easter's Master and Mistress' consent to let Ellec take Easter for wife. In fact they would not agree to give her up until Mr. Robinson signed a contract to pay a bonus of several hundred dollars. He said they were obliged to ask for this because they had wasted all of Easter's working time, since she became old enough to work; having her trained in the arts of cooking sewing, and spinning. They had expected to sell her someday at a very high bid and did not feel that they could give her away. They told Mr. R. that they would call it a square deal if he agreed to let Ellec come to their plantation with Easter to stay. At which Mr. R.

replied, not for a half dozen women slaves would he depart with B. B.

So sometime in A. D. 1834, the Second Generation Marriage took place, Alexander Sioux Robinson, (Big Branch) an Overseer Slave of George Robinson and Agnes Robinson Chamberlyn was married to Easter Elizabeth Bland, Slave girl of Richard Bland, Second. All of the County of Brunswick in the state of Virginia. The Bride and Groom resided on the Robinson and Smith plantation.

~//~

Chapter 14
Ann's Afterthoughts

GRANDMA! AS I read the inside cover of your composition notebook, I saw this format and the information that you filled in:

S t e r l i n g
NOTE BOOK
Property of <u>Mrs. P. W. Eastman Sr.</u>
School <u>A. D. 1952–3–4</u>
No. 3966

FAMILY NAME   GIVEN NAME
Section <u>Book #1 of the lineage of J. J. Eastman</u>
Book # a1: *Winna to*
   Alexander Sioux Robinson to
   Ciney Sioux Robinson Jones to
   Julia Jones Eastman and the Eastman Clan [*]
*[Philip Walter, Jr., Rebecca Juanita, Esther Elizabeth, Julius Dunbar, Sr., Oliver Cromwell, Ciney Mae, William Barlow, Sylvester Joseph, Candace Yvette, Harold Vernon]

The Eastman Clan consisted of my father, Philip Walter Eastman, Jr., your first born; then from him and my mother Anna Byrd Eastman, came me. I was also loved and spoiled by all of your sons and daughters, my aunts and uncles. Thank you, Grandma for your love and caring, especially since I was so hardheaded, especially about coming in from playing outside too long after elementary school days at P. S. 99 on Stebbins Ave. during the late 1940s. At family gatherings my cousins and I thought we were hot stuff as we enjoyed the glass of Pepsi Cola with a sip of Manischewitz grape wine that you used to slip into the Pepsi for me and David (son of Esther), and Julius, Jr. (son of Julius, Sr.). It was probably just about a half a teaspoon now that I think of it.

While you were remembering and compiling these salient and connected parts of our ancestry, I was struggling with handwriting exercises in cursive, trying hard not to continue to just print by hand. I stopped the transcription of Book I at your page 93. You have other historical details about specific events which I wished I could have had in my history books at school. I was in a special two-year fast track class at Herman Ridder Junior High School, Grades 7–9, near Boston Road in the Bronx. I was the only colored girl (one other colored boy) in my 7SP class. Reading thought-provoking essays and lyrical poetry with no samples from Black writers, did not prevent me from auditioning to be the comedic maid in the school play. I chose that part because I didn't think I would be chosen for the female lead no matter how well I "knew" I could act. I did recognize that the maid's part would steal the show with her lines of comedy (and it did!) The Director said yes, but my Dad said

NO. He had absorbed his father's spirit of pride and seriousness, and zero tolerance for anything that smacked of racism.

We are still dealing with racism, Grandma Julia, but we have the foundations of faith, love, and strength, passed down to us from Edyth on, to live, laugh, and struggle; and many times, we do overcome. My dear cousins, the next generation, it's up to you to continue our history and legacy.

~//~

Family Photos

L-R Rebecca, Julia's Daughter; Anna Byrd Eastman, Author Ann Tyler's Mother; Baby Ann (Author); Grandma Julia May Jones Eastman

L-R Grandma Julia; Author Ann "Junie" Tyler; Anna

Philip, Jr., Julia's Firstborn, Father of Ann Tyler

Oliver, Son of Julia

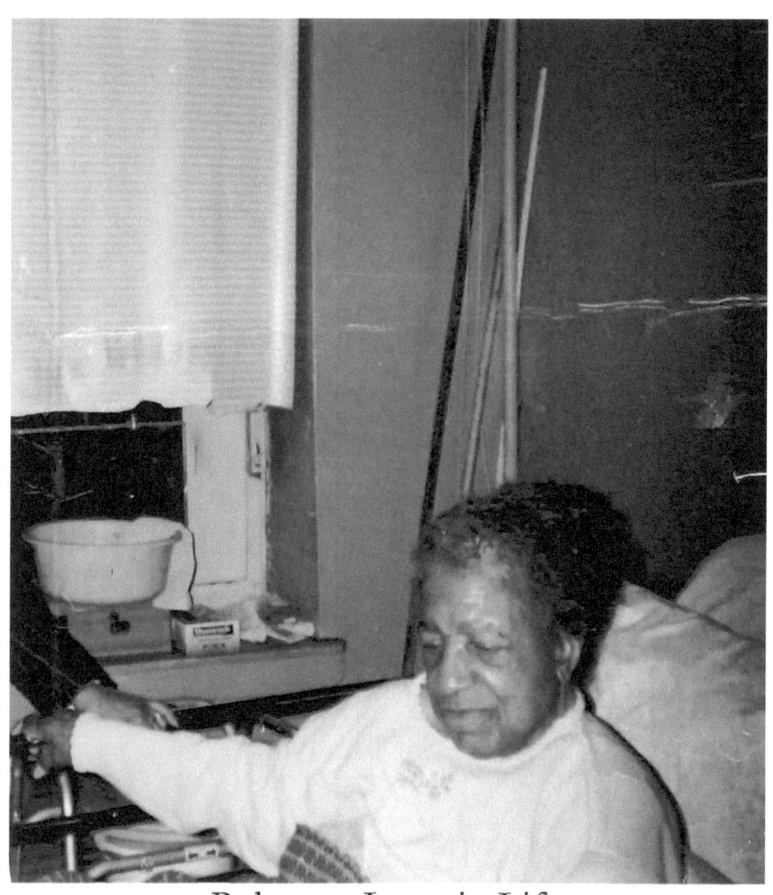

Rebecca, Later in Life

Julius, Son of Julia

"Gerry", Son of Julius and Glen Evans,
Son of Gerry

Anna and Philip, Jr., Parents of Ann Tyler

Ann and her Granddaughter,
Jeanna Yvette Tyler

Bill P. Ellison, Son of Ann Tyler, and Ann's Mother, Anna, Later in Life

Annette Ellison, Daughter of Ann Tyler, and
Robert "Bebop" Tyler, Son of Ann

Robert and his firstborn infant,
Termaine Tyler Creek

L-R Machelle, John, Son of David Lisbon, Sr.; June, Distant Cousin of Julia; David Lisbon, Sr., Julia's Grandson

Younger days in Buffalo with
Dr. Yvonne Scruggs-Leftwich "Bonnie," A
beloved Byrd cousin and mentor,
and Dr. Ann Y. Eastman Ellison Tyler "Junie"

Annette, Bill with Ann Tyler

John Lisbon, Son of David Lisbon, Sr.

> (Identifications)
>
> ① of 1)
> continued from a(92)
>
> 93
>
> Now concerning the locket spoken of on page 14 of this book, Kheenee Sioux had gone back, after he had rescued Winna from drowning, to the spot where she fell in the stream and picked up the socks which Winna was knitting and carried them to his wig. and used some of the thread with which she was knitting and intertwined it with a thread like wisp of his hair and had fastened it, in a heart shape figure, to a 4 inch square piece of chamois skin, and in the center of the heart was engraved the two words — Kheenee Sioux — which when he had asked Winna her name, as mentioned on page 13 of this book, and had obtained a wisp of her hair, he went to his wig and made another locket in the same shape and size as the one he had given Winna, and in the center was the word — Winna — . The next time he saw Winna he asked her to let him have the ensign he had given her so that he could weave the two together. She had him unfasten it at the back and slip it

Sample Page From Grandma Julia's Original Notebook

~ / / ~

APPENDIX A

<u>Tragedy of Wayside Brook 7B</u>[1]
by Candace Yvette Eastman

One day a maid with head bowed down
Walked the Bridge of Wayside Brook
Her clothing was a long, black gown
And sad and sorrowful was her look
For on the morrow she was to wed
A man, a stranger from overseas
For so it was her Sire had said
And hardened his heart to all her pleas
This stranger was an evil man
His slanting eyes were fierce, and red
And it was said he roamed the land
When all good folks had gone a-bed
In vain the maid with tearful eyes
Implored her sire as I have told
But her father's heart was no great size
And he loved the stranger for his gold.
So from his house the maiden fled
And came at last to Wayside Brook
And I believe before I've said

That sad and sorrowful was her look
Then her aching heart was eased, and through
A prayer for death straight from her soul
For ne'er would she be wedded to
This evil stranger and his gold.
So from the bridge the maid did leap
The swirling waves closed o'er her head
And she was claimed by the Gods of the Deep
Her prayer was answered—The maiden was dead
And yet, 'tis said, on a stormy night
When the wind does whistle and wail around
The bridge is lit by an eerie light
And the maid walks there in her trailing gown.

~//~

GLOSSARY OF THE SLAVE DIALECT
For This Edition

A

Ah(m): I('m, am)
anudder: another
arter: after
ax: ask

B

becase: because
bahn: barn
befo: before
brudder: brother

C

caus(e): because
Ciney: also Chenne
clar: declare
con: corn
controll: control
cuden: couldn't
cum, cummin: come, coming

D

dat: that
Dats: That's
de: the, it
dem: them
den: then
dere: there
dese: these
deth: death
dey: they
dis: this
don: don't, done
dregged: dragged

E

ebery: every
eberywhar: everywhere
Edith: also Eady, Edyth
ef: if
eny: any
evah: ever

F

fambly: family
fer: for
fishermon: fisherman
fo, fo': for, before

fren, frin: friend
fust: first

G

gi': give
git, gitten: get, getting
Grany: Granny, Grandmother
gwinter: going to

H

heah: here
heme: him
hit: it
holerdy: holiday
hunny: Honey
hur: her

J

joyfull: joyful

K

keah, kere: care
Kheenee: Khee-nee, Keenee, Ken
kud: could

L

Lawd: Lord
Lawsy, Laws!: Lord!
leck: like
Looka: Look, look at
loss: lost

M

marsa, marsa's: Master, Master's—plantation owner
Marse, Marster: Master
masa, massa: Master
mene: mean (indicating)
minature: miniature
Missipi: Mississippi
mity: mighty
monin: morning
mought, mout: might
moun: more than

N

Naw: No
Norf: North
No, noe: know
nowhar: nowhere
Nuffin': Nothing

O

ony: only

P

paralized: paralyzed
po, poh: poor
posimmon: persimmon
purty: pretty

S

sed: said
seganku: skunk pelt (Possibly New England Algonquian Language)
shakey: shaky
squelin': squealing
sho: sure
skert: scared
slep: slept
Suh: Sir
sum: some
swar: swear

T

tahm, tarm: time
tawk: talk

ter: to
termarrah: tomorrow
thang: thing
Thankee: Thanks
tremolous(ly): tremulous(ly)

U

Uh huh: Yes
um: to the, him
un: and
untill: until
us: us, our

V

Villian: Villain

W

Wal: well
watah: water
wen: went
whar: where
whupped: whipped
wid: with
Winna: also Wina, Wenna, Rowina
wone: won't, weren't
woz: was

Y

Yessum: Yes M'am
yo', yos: you, your

~ / / ~

INDEX

Africans, 2
Alexander Sioux, 58
American Indian, 13
Army, 62
banjos, 67
Big Branch, 68, 72
bearskin, 10, 22
Bland, Easter, 68, 72
Brunswick, County of, 3, 72
Ciney, 2, 73
deerskin, 10
Dismal Swamp, 63, 64
drums, 67
Eastman, i, 74
Edith, 2, 3, 11
Ellic Sioux, 2
Emancipation, 1
fur, 17
generations, 18
hemstitch, 30
Henderson, 2
Indian, 8, 16, 45, 58
Jew's harp, 67
Ken, 17, 64
Kheenee Sioux, 24, 31
knitting, 6, 12

Leadbetter's Ball, 42
legacy, 75
Lena, 11, 34
locket, 12, 13
Marriage, 72
Missippi, 28, 29, 32
Negroes, 61, 64
nutberry beads, 67
pallet, 10, 46
pickaniny, 23
plantation, 2, 22, 31, 70
purling, 6
Redman, 10, 24
Robinson, 3, 58, 62
Robinson-Smith, 4
Rowina, 2
slaves, 4, 72
sling, 31
squirrel, 19, 37
tallow, 11
tribe, 13, 58
Virginia, State of, 3, 72
Willa, 2, 70
Winna, 2, 28, 46
Yankee Raiders, 63

~//~